PIANO THEORY

T0065954

ISBN 978-1-4803-6318-2

7777 W. BLUEMOUND RD. P.O. BOX 13819 MILWAUKEE, WI 53213

In Australia Contact:
Hal Leonard Australia Pty. Ltd.
4 Lentara Court
Cheltenham, Victoria, 3192 Australia
Email: ausadmin@halleonard.com.au

Visit Hal Leonard Online at
www.halleonard.com

To the Student

I wrote these books with you in mind. As a young student I often wondered how completing theory workbooks would make me a better musician. The theory work often seemed separate from the music I was playing. My goal in *Essential Elements Piano Theory* is to provide you with the tools you will need to compose, improvise, play classical and popular music, or to better understand any other musical pursuit you might enjoy. In each "Musical Mastery" section of this book you will experience creative applications of the theory you have learned. The "Ear Training" pages will be completed with your teacher at the lesson. In this series you will begin to learn the building blocks of music, which make it possible for you to have fun at the piano. A practical understanding of theory enables you to see what is possible in music. I wish you all the best on your journey as you learn the language of music!

Sincerely,
Mona Rejino

To the Teacher

I believe that knowledge of theory is most beneficial when a concept is followed directly by a musical application. In *Essential Elements Piano Theory*, learning theory becomes far more than completing worksheets. Students have the opportunity to see why learning a particular concept can help them become a better pianist right away. They can also see how the knowledge of musical patterns and chord progressions will enable them to be creative in their own musical pursuits: composing, arranging, improvising, playing classical and popular music, accompanying, or any other.

A free download of the *Teacher's Answer Key* is available at www.halleonard.com/eeptheory6answer.

Acknowledgements

I would like to thank Hal Leonard Corporation for providing me the opportunity to put these theoretical thoughts down on paper and share them with others. I owe a debt of gratitude to Jennifer Linn, who has helped with this project every step of the way. These books would not have been possible without the support of my family: To my husband, Richard, for his wisdom and amazing ability to solve dilemmas; to my children, Maggie and Adam, for helping me think outside the box.

TABLE OF CONTENTS

REVIEW

1. Add bar lines to each rhythm below.

2. Identify each triad by writing the correct Roman numeral in the box. Choose from **I**, **i**, **IV**, **iv** and **V**.

| G minor | C Major | E minor | D Major | A minor |

3. Draw the root position triads indicated in each Major or minor key. Use whole notes.

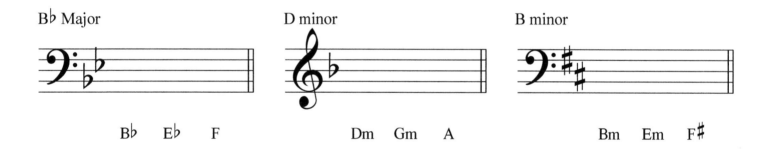

| Bb Major | D minor | B minor |

Bb   Eb   F   Dm Gm A   Bm Em F#

4. Name each triad by writing the letter name of its root in the box. If the triad is minor, add a small **m** after the root letter name.

5. Draw the root position, 1st inversion and 2nd inversion triads in each measure using whole notes. Name the key signature.

_____ Major

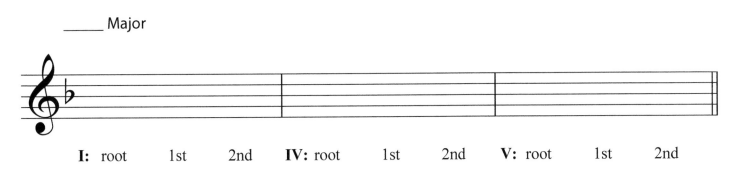

I: root   1st   2nd   IV: root   1st   2nd   V: root   1st   2nd

6. For each chord below:

   a. Fill in the root note.

   b. Name its position (**root** for root position, **1st** for 1st inversion and **2nd** for 2nd inversion.)

   c. Circle **M** for Major or **m** for minor. *The first one is done for you.*

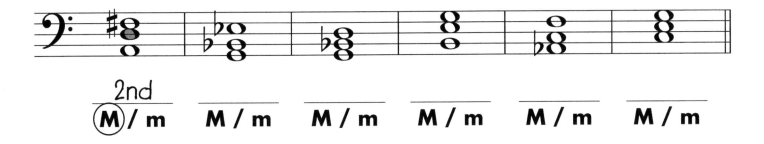

_2nd_ _____ _____ _____ _____ _____

(M)/ m   M / m   M / m   M / m   M / m   M / m

7. Name each Major key signature and its relative minor key signature.

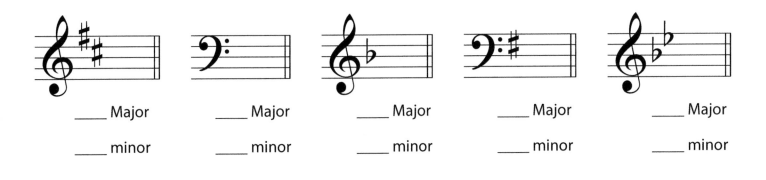

____ Major   ____ Major   ____ Major   ____ Major   ____ Major

____ minor   ____ minor   ____ minor   ____ minor   ____ minor

8. Fill in the blanks.

   a. The _____ minor scale follows the key signature, with no changes.

   b. The seventh note is raised a half step ascending and descending in the _____ minor scale.

   c. The sixth and seventh notes are raised a half step ascending, then are lowered descending in the _____ minor scale.

9. Add accidentals to complete each scale.

E Natural Minor

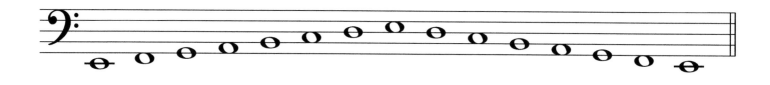

A Harmonic Minor

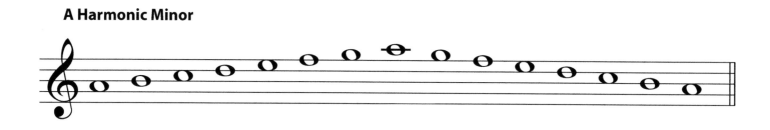

B Melodic Minor

D Harmonic Minor

Time Signatures and Rhythm

COMMON TIME is another name for $\frac{4}{4}$.

$$\mathbf{C} = \frac{4}{4}$$

= 4 beats in a measure

= quarter note (♩) gets one beat

CUT TIME is another name for $\frac{2}{2}$.

$$\mathbf{\Cutc} = \frac{2}{2}$$

= 2 beats in a measure

= half note (♩) gets one beat

Pieces in **C** are counted "in 4."

Pieces in **¢** are counted "in 2."

Clap and count:

C	♩		♩	♩	♩	♩	♩	♩	♩	♩	♩		o			
	1	- 2	3	4	1	2	3	4	1	2	3 - 4		1 - 2 - 3 - 4			
¢	1	and	2	and	1	and	2	and	1	and	2	and	1	and	2	and

1. Write the counts below each measure, then clap and count the rhythm. Use a + sign for the word "and."

2. Add bar lines to this rhythm. Write in the counts. Choose one key on the piano and play the rhythm while counting aloud.

In **4/4** time: ♪ A sixteenth note = 1/4 beat of sound

♪ A sixteenth rest = 1/4 beat of silence

Two or more sixteenth notes are joined by two beams.

3. Add two flags to the quarter notes to make sixteenth notes.

4. Add two beams to the quarter notes to make pairs of sixteenth notes.

5. Add two beams to the quarter notes to make groups of four sixteenth notes.

6. Trace the sixteenth rest, then draw four more.

♪

7. Clap and count the rhythms below, keeping a steady beat.

The following rhythm patterns combine eighth and sixteenth notes.

Clap and count:

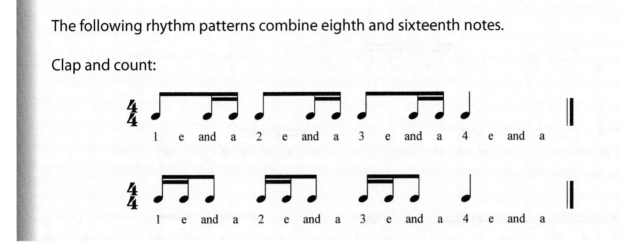

8. Write the counts below each measure, using a + sign for the word "and." Choose one key on the piano and play each example while counting aloud.

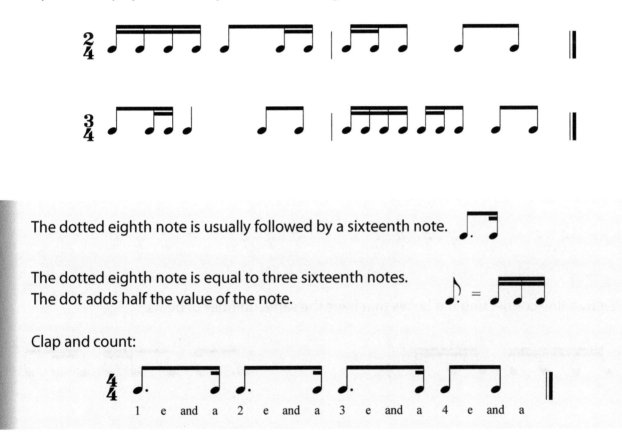

The dotted eighth note is usually followed by a sixteenth note.

The dotted eighth note is equal to three sixteenth notes.
The dot adds half the value of the note.

Clap and count:

9. Write the counts below each measure. Choose one key on the piano and play each example while counting aloud.

10. Draw bar lines where they are needed.

11. In each box draw one note that equals the total value of the other notes.

12. In each box draw one rest that equals the total value of the sixteenth rests.

$$\overset{\text{-}}{\gamma}\ \overset{\text{-}}{\gamma}\ =\qquad\overset{\text{-}}{\gamma}\ \overset{\text{-}}{\gamma}\ \overset{\text{-}}{\gamma}\ \overset{\text{-}}{\gamma}\ =\qquad\overset{\text{-}}{\gamma}\ \overset{\text{-}}{\gamma}\ \overset{\text{-}}{\gamma}\ \overset{\text{-}}{\gamma}\ \overset{\text{-}}{\gamma}\ \overset{\text{-}}{\gamma}\ \overset{\text{-}}{\gamma}\ \overset{\text{-}}{\gamma}\ =$$

13. Draw a line connecting the boxes that have the same number of beats.

Major Sharp Key Signatures and Scales

Keys are related by Perfect 5ths. Begin with the Key of C (no sharps or flats) and go up a 5th to the Key of G (one sharp.) Go up a 5th from G to the Key of D (two sharps.) The pattern continues through all the sharp keys.

UP BY PERFECT FIFTHS

C	G	D	A	E	B	F#	C#
0	1 sharp	2 sharps	3 sharps	4 sharps	5 sharps	6 sharps	7 sharps

1. Fill in the blanks with the correct letters and numbers.

   a. A 5th above C is the Key of _____ which has _____ sharp.

   b. A 5th above G is the Key of _____ which has _____ sharps.

   c. A 5th above D is the Key of _____ which has _____ sharps.

   d. A 5th above A is the Key of _____ which has _____ sharps.

   e. A 5th above E is the Key of _____ which has _____ sharps.

   f. A 5th above B is the Key of _____ which has _____ sharps.

   g. A 5th above F# is the Key of _____ which has _____ sharps.

The **ORDER OF SHARPS** starts on F and goes up by intervals of a 5th.

F C G D A E B

2. Name the order of sharps.

Sharps in a key signature are always written in the same order on the staff.

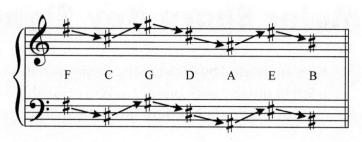

F   C   G   D   A   E   B

3. Write the order of sharps in each blank measure.

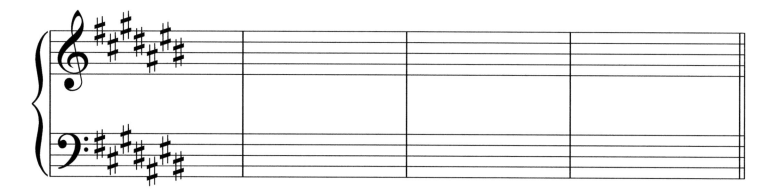

To identify a Major sharp key:
   a. Name the last sharp to the right.
   b. Go up a half step.

E Major

4. Circle the last sharp in each example. Think of the note name that is a half step up from this sharp, then write the name of the Major key signature in the box. *The first one is done for you.*

D Major

5. Add the correct sharps to form these Major scales. Mark the half steps with a curved line. Draw the key signature for each scale. *The first one is done for you.*

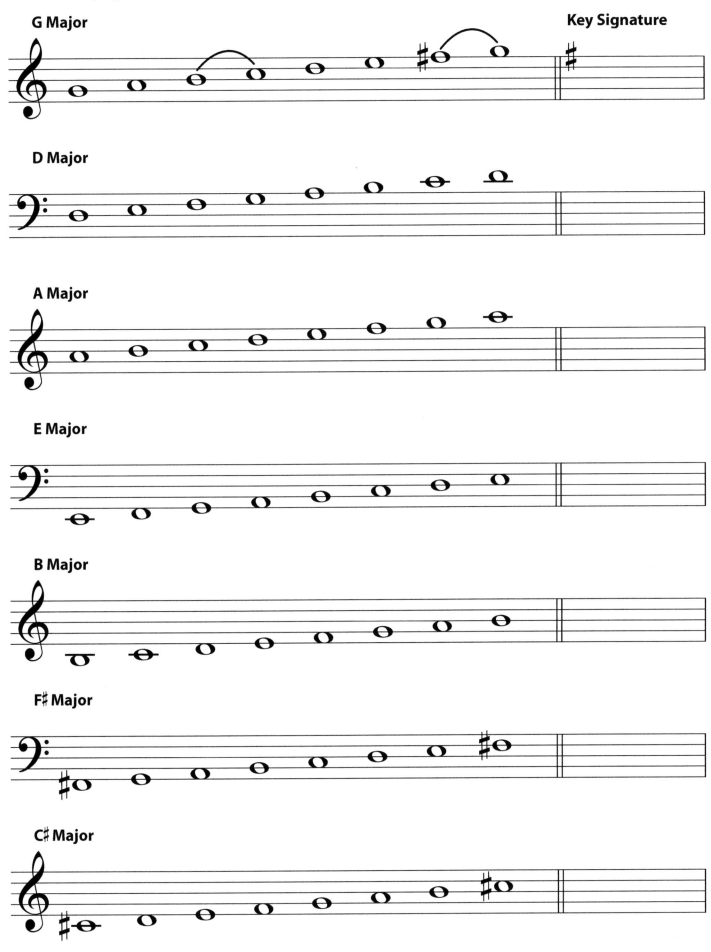

Major Flat Key Signatures and Scales

Begin with the Key of C and go down a Perfect 5th to the Key of F (one flat.) Go down a 5th from F to the Key of B♭ (two flats.) The pattern continues through all the flat keys.

DOWN BY PERFECT FIFTHS

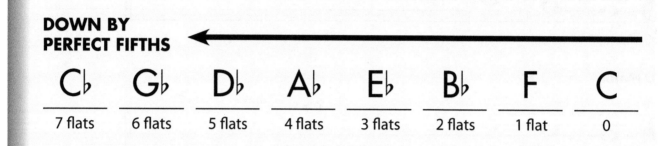

C♭	G♭	D♭	A♭	E♭	B♭	F	C
7 flats	6 flats	5 flats	4 flats	3 flats	2 flats	1 flat	0

1. Fill in the blanks with the correct letters and numbers.

   a. A 5th below C is the key of _____ which has _____ flat.

   b. A 5th below F is the key of _____ which has _____ flats.

   c. A 5th below B♭ is the key of _____ which has _____ flats.

   d. A 5th below E♭ is the key of _____ which has _____ flats.

   e. A 5th below A♭ is the key of _____ which has _____ flats.

   f. A 5th below D♭ is the key of _____ which has _____ flats.

   g. A 5th below G♭ is the key of _____ which has _____ flats.

The **ORDER OF FLATS** starts on B and goes down by intervals of a 5th.

B E A D G C F

The order of flats is the order of sharps backwards.

2. Name the order of flats.

   _____ _____ _____ _____ _____ _____ _____

14

Flats in a key signature are always written in the same order on the staff.

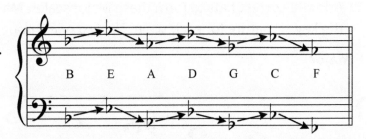

B E A D G C F

3. Write the order of flats in each blank measure.

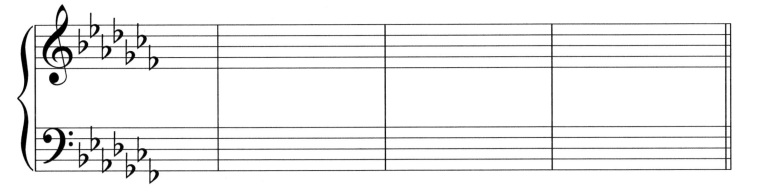

To identify a Major flat key:

   a. Name the next to the last flat.

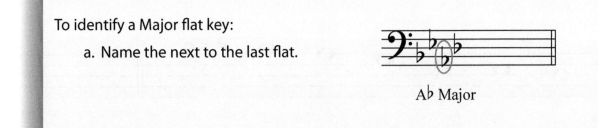

A♭ Major

4. Circle the next to the last flat in each example. Think of its name, then write the name of the Major key signature in the box. The Key of F Major with a B♭ must be memorized. *The first one is done for you.*

B♭ Major

5. Add the correct flats to form these Major scales. Mark the half steps with a curved line. Draw
   the key signature for each scale. *The first one is done for you.*

F Major   **Key Signature**

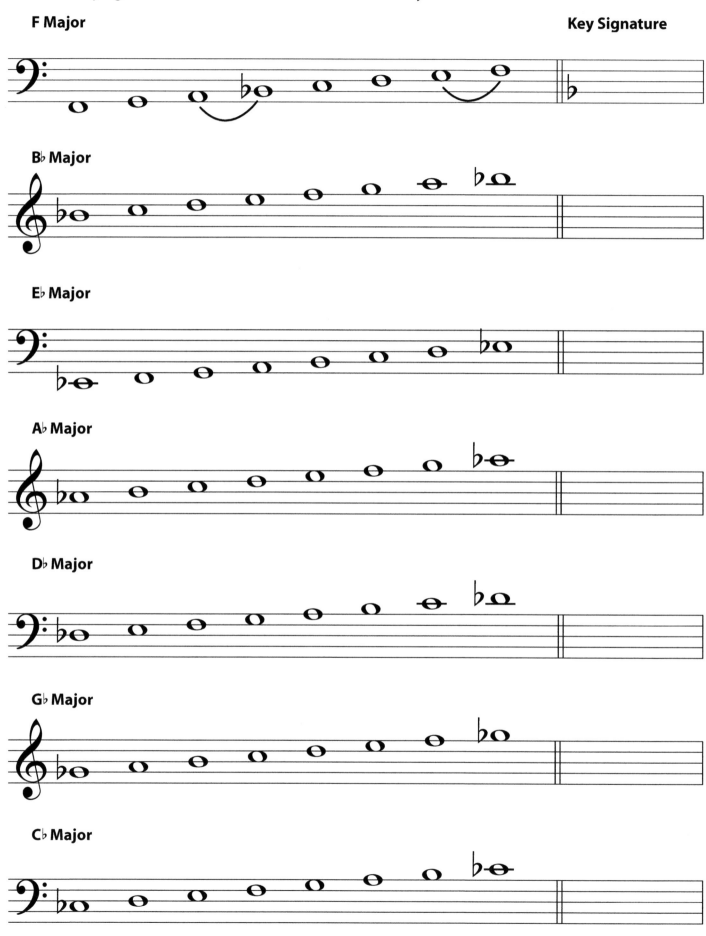

B♭ Major

E♭ Major

A♭ Major

D♭ Major

G♭ Major

C♭ Major

Major Circle of Fifths

The **CIRCLE OF FIFTHS** is a diagram showing the relationship between key signatures.

The keys are arranged a Perfect 5th apart. Moving clockwise from the Key of C Major at the top, each key signature adds one sharp. Moving counterclockwise from the Key of C Major, each key signature adds one flat.

The keys at the bottom are enharmonic keys. They sound the same, but are written and named differently.

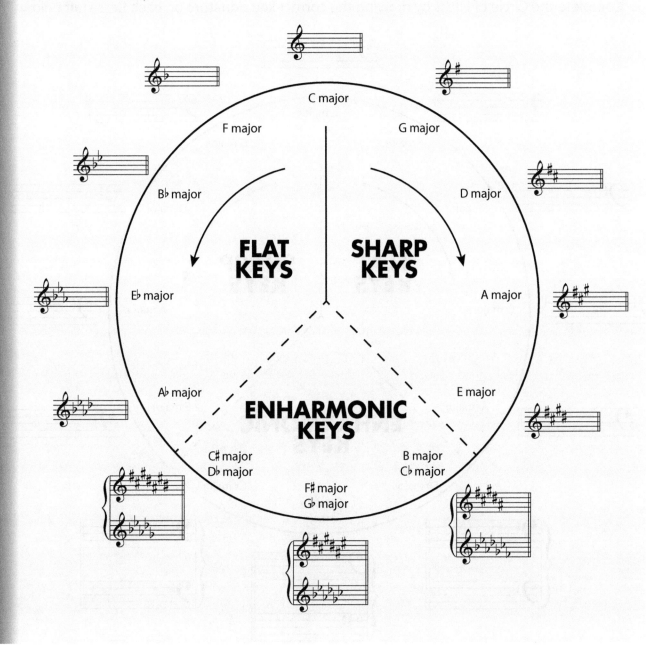

1. Name the order of sharps.

_____ _____ _____ _____ _____ _____ _____

2. Name the order of flats.

_____ _____ _____ _____ _____ _____ _____

3. Complete the Circle of Fifths by drawing the correct key signature on each bass staff below.

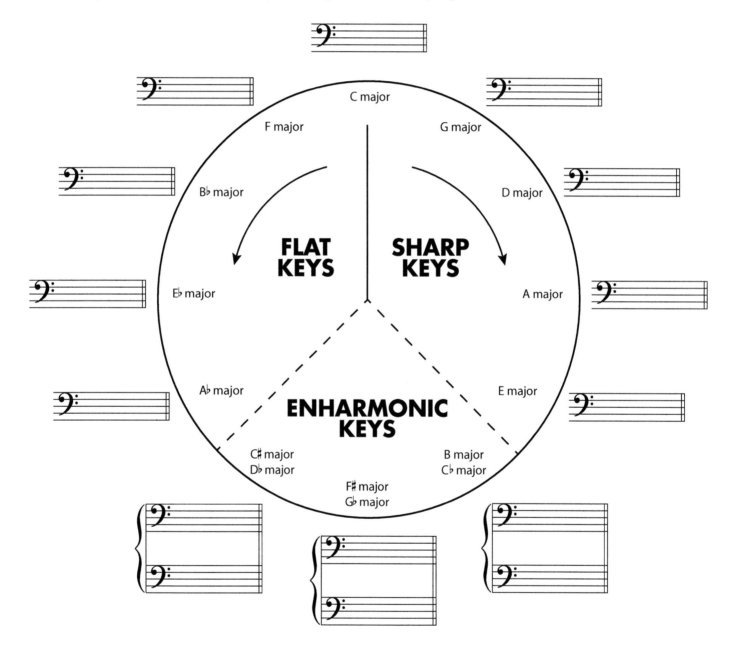

MUSICAL MASTERY

Ear Training

1. You will hear one rhythm from each pair. Circle the rhythm you hear.

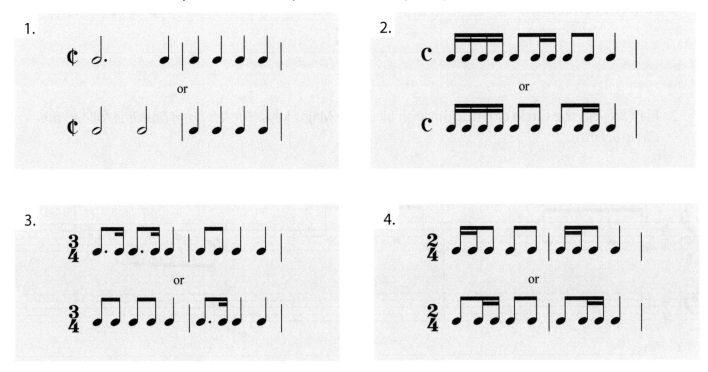

2. You will hear intervals of a 2nd, 3rd, 5th, 7th or 8th played in broken and blocked form. Name the correct interval in each blank.

   1. _____   2. _____   3. _____   4. _____   5. _____   6. _____

3. You will hear six scales ascending and descending. Identify each scale as Major (**Maj.**) or harmonic minor (**har. min.**).

   1. _____   2. _____   3. _____

   4. _____   5. _____   6. _____

Reading Mastery: Playing Around the Circle of Fifths

1. Complete the linear Circle of Fifths by filling in the blanks.

Down by Perfect 5ths ⟵⟶ Up by Perfect 5ths

C

___ ___ ___ ___ ___ ___   ___ ___ ___ ___ ___ ___ ___

2. Play around the Circle of Fifths through all of the Major keys. *The left hand bass line follows the Circle of Fifths.*

Rhythm Mastery

1. Draw one note in the empty box to balance each scale.

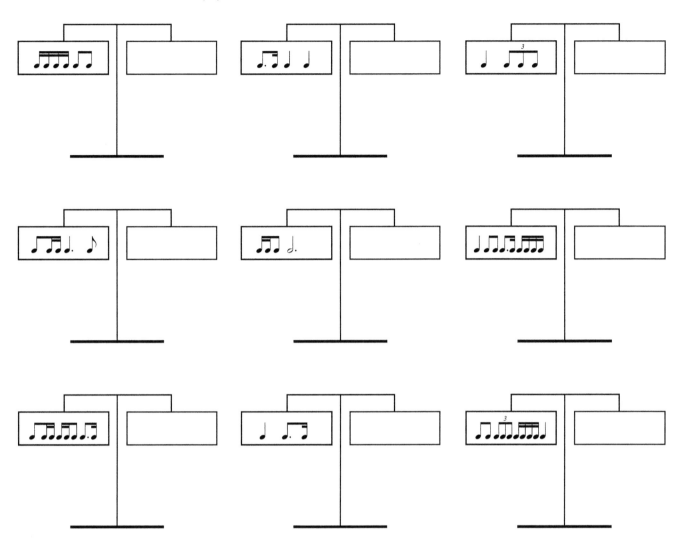

2. Draw one rest in the empty box to balance each scale.

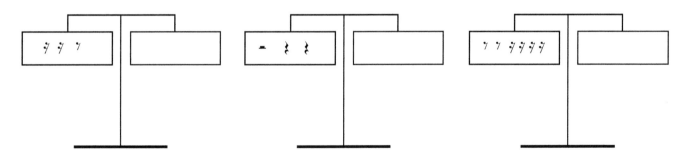

Perfect and Major Intervals

Two types of intervals are found within a Major scale:

PERFECT and **MAJOR**

The interval between the tonic note and the unison, 4th, 5th and octave is called a
Perfect interval.

The interval between the tonic note and the 2nd, 3rd, 6th and 7th is called a
Major interval.

Key of C Major

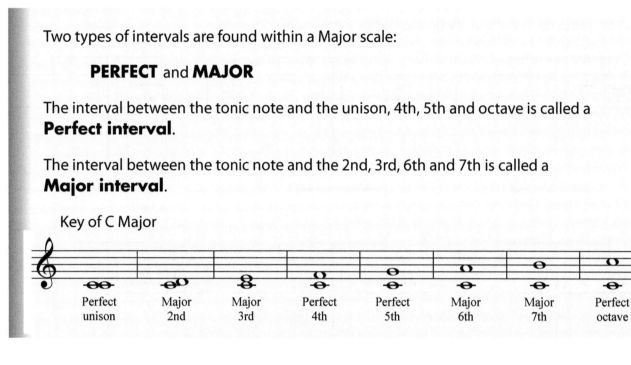

1. Identify the key signature in the blank. Name the harmonic intervals of the scale. Use **P** for
Perfect and **M** for Major. *The first and last measures are done for you.*

Key of _____ Major

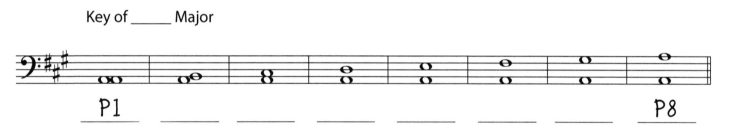

2. Identify the key signature in the blank. Name the melodic intervals of the scale.

Key of _____ Major

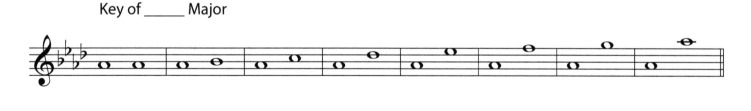

3. Identify the Major key signature, then name the intervals of the scale.

Key of _____ Major

Key of _____ Major

Key of _____ Major

Key of _____ Major

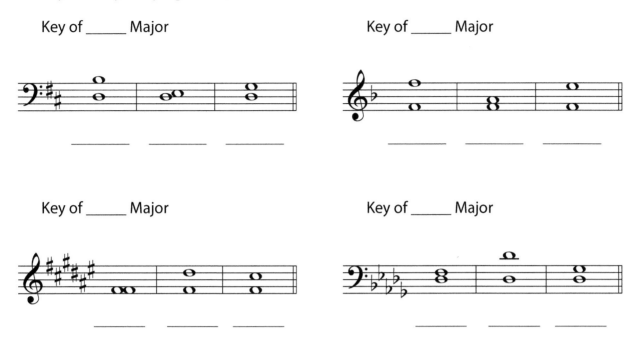

_____ _____ _____   _____ _____ _____

_____ _____ _____   _____ _____ _____

4. Name the following intervals. Consider the lowest note in each interval as the tonic note of that Major scale.

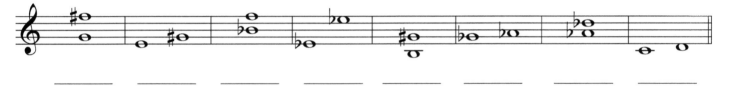

_____ _____ _____ _____ _____ _____ _____ _____

5. Draw a note above the given note to complete the harmonic intervals. Add accidentals where needed. Remember the Major scale to which each interval belongs. *The first one is done for you.*

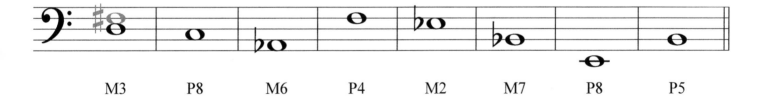

 M3 P8 M6 P4 M2 M7 P8 P5

Augmented and Diminished Triads

A **MAJOR TRIAD** has a Major 3rd on the bottom and a minor 3rd on top.

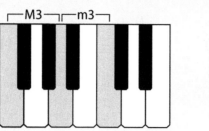

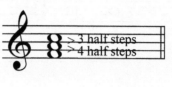

A **MINOR TRIAD** has a minor 3rd on the bottom and a Major 3rd on top.

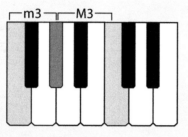

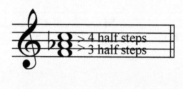

An **AUGMENTED TRIAD** is made up of two Major 3rds.

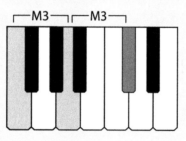

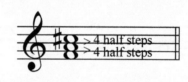

A **DIMINISHED TRIAD** is made up of two minor 3rds.

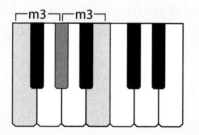

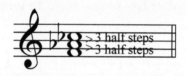

An Augmented triad is formed by raising the top note (5th) of a Major triad a half step.

A diminished triad is formed by lowering the top note (5th) of a minor triad a half step.

1. Draw an Augmented triad after each Major triad, then play each chord.

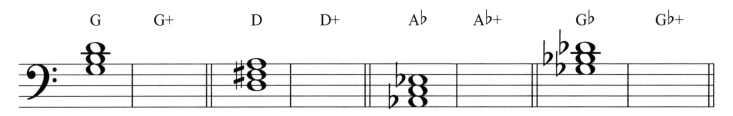

2. Draw the following Augmented triads. *Root position triads are always made up of intervals of a 3rd.*

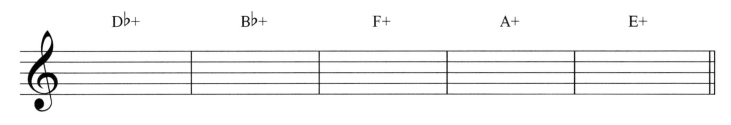

3. Draw a diminished triad after each minor triad, then play each chord.

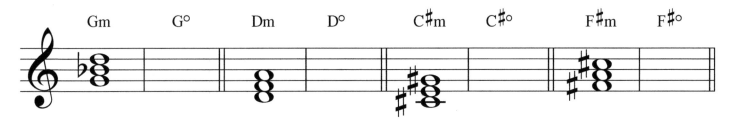

4. Draw the following diminished triads. *Root position triads are always made up of intervals of a 3rd.*

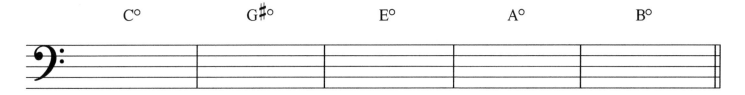

5. Identify the following triads by letter name and quality: Major (**M**), minor (**m**), Augmented (**+**) or diminished (**°**). *The first one is done for you.*

Cb+

UNIT 8

Cadences and Chord Progressions

A **CADENCE** is the combination of chords that ends a phrase or section of music. Cadences provide resting points in music.

The following cadences use primary triads:

Authentic Cadence:	V to I	(Dominant to Tonic)
Plagal Cadence:	IV to I	(Subdominant to Tonic)
Half Cadence:	IV to V or I to V	(ends on the Dominant)

AUTHENTIC **PLAGAL** **HALF**

The following cadences use primary triads:

Key of C Major

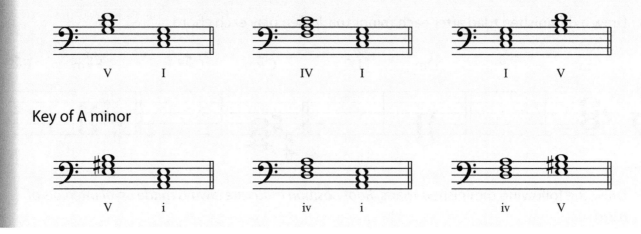

| V | I | IV | I | I | V |

Key of A minor

| V | i | iv | i | iv | V |

1. Fill in the blanks with the correct Roman numerals for each cadence. Name the type of cadence in each box.

Key of F Major

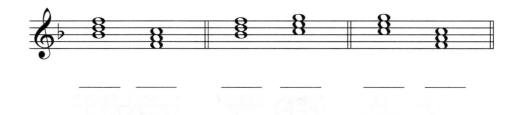

_____ _____   _____ _____   _____ _____

Key of E Major

_____ _____ _____ _____ _____ _____

Key of G minor

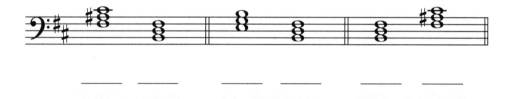

_____ _____ _____ _____ _____ _____

Key of B minor

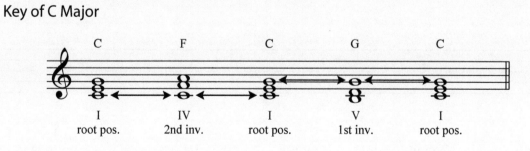

_____ _____ _____ _____ _____ _____

A **CHORD PROGRESSION** is the movement from one chord to another. Chord Progressions often mix root position and inverted chords, which creates smooth sounding progressions and makes them easier to play. **COMMON TONES** are notes shared between chords in a progression.

Key of C Major

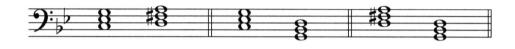

2. Write the I – IV – I – V – I chord progression in the given key. Draw arrows to show the common tones between chords. Identify the missing chord symbols or Roman numerals in the boxes.

Key of G Major

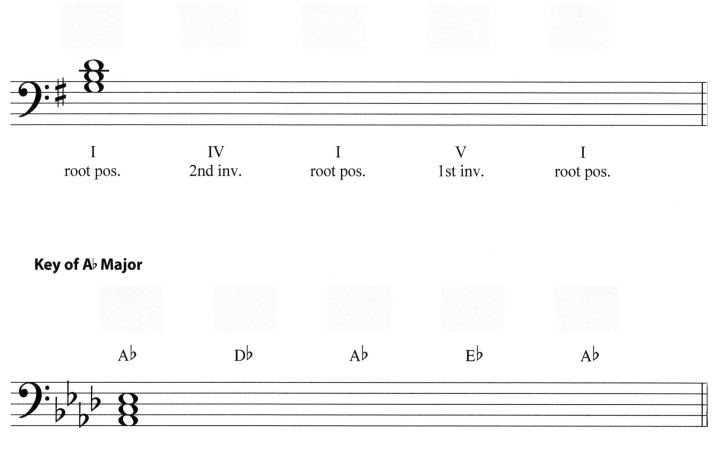

| I | IV | I | V | I |
| root pos. | 2nd inv. | root pos. | 1st inv. | root pos. |

Key of A♭ Major

| A♭ | D♭ | A♭ | E♭ | A♭ |

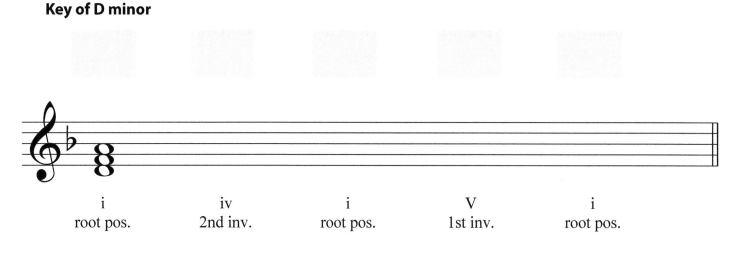

| root pos. | 2nd inv. | root pos. | 1st inv. | root pos. |

3. Write the i – iv – i – V – i chord progression in the given key. Draw arrows to show the common tones between chords. Identify the missing chord symbols in the boxes.

Key of D minor

| i | iv | i | V | i |
| root pos. | 2nd inv. | root pos. | 1st inv. | root pos. |

4. Play all of the chord progressions above.

Dominant Seventh Chords

A **SEVENTH CHORD** is made up of four notes: root, third, fifth and seventh.

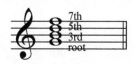

A seventh chord built on the fifth degree (dominant) of the scale is called the **DOMINANT SEVENTH CHORD** (V7). In root position it consists of a Major triad plus a minor third.

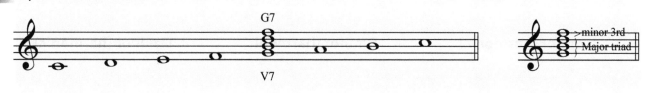

1. Draw a dominant seventh chord on the 5th note of each scale. Place its letter name in the box above the chord. Add accidentals where needed.

D Major

F Major

A minor (harmonic)

G minor (harmonic)

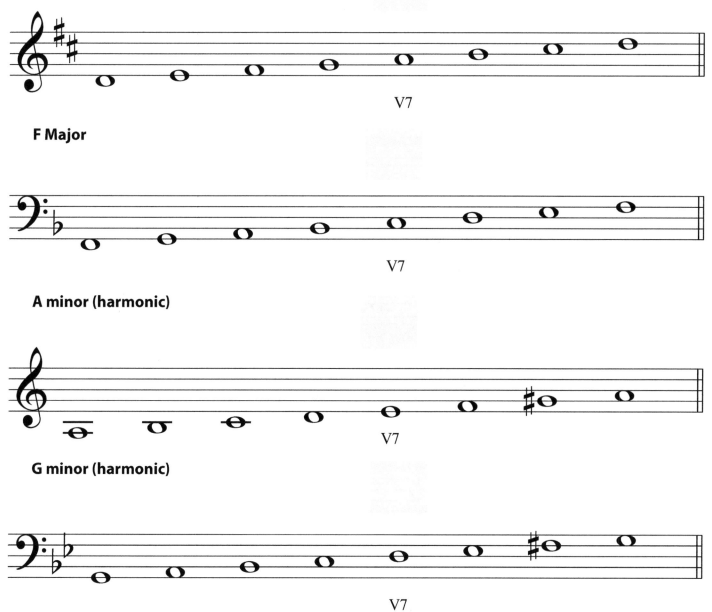

2. Draw the V7 chord for each key. Place its letter name in the box. *The dominant seventh chord is built on the dominant note in that key.*

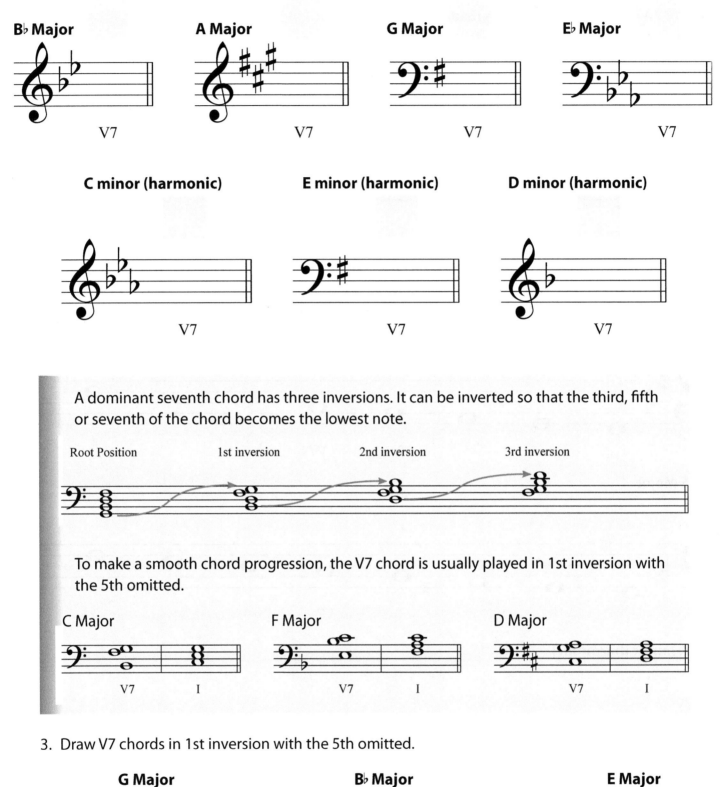

A dominant seventh chord has three inversions. It can be inverted so that the third, fifth or seventh of the chord becomes the lowest note.

To make a smooth chord progression, the V7 chord is usually played in 1st inversion with the 5th omitted.

3. Draw V7 chords in 1st inversion with the 5th omitted.

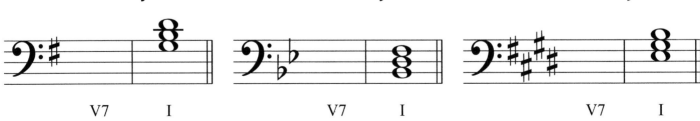

30

4. Two chords are missing in each chord progression. Draw the missing chords on the staff. The I or i chord will be in root position, the IV or iv chord in 2nd inversion, and the V7 chord in 1st inversion with the 5th omitted. Each chord will share one common tone.

C Major

I   IV   V7   I

A minor (harmonic)

i   iv   V7   i

E♭ Major

I   IV   V7   I

G minor (harmonic)

i   iv   V7   i

B Major

I   IV   V7   I

MUSICAL MASTERY

Ear Training

1. You will hear four measures of rhythmic dictation. Fill in the blank measures with the rhythm you hear.

2. You will hear six triads played in broken and blocked form. Identify them as Major, minor or Augmented.

    1. _____   2. _____   3. _____

    4. _____   5. _____   6. _____

3. You will hear one interval from each pair. Circle the interval you hear.

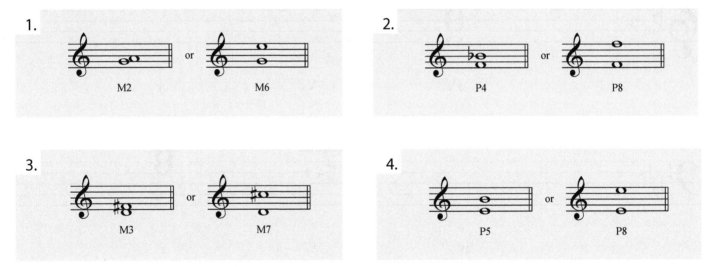

4. You will hear four scales ascending and descending. Circle the type of scale that you hear.

    a. Major   harmonic minor   melodic minor

    b. Major   harmonic minor   melodic minor

    c. Major   harmonic minor   melodic minor

    d. Major   harmonic minor   melodic minor

Chordal Accompaniments

Create a chordal accompaniment by harmonizing the following melodies.

1. Name the key signature.

2. Play each melody.

3. Using the Roman numerals as a guide, write the correct blocked primary triads in the boxes. Use a smooth chord progression.

4. Combine the melody and accompaniment, and play each example.

Key of _____ minor

    i   iv   V7   i

Key of _____ Major

  I   IV   I   V7   I   IV   V7   I

Key of _____ minor

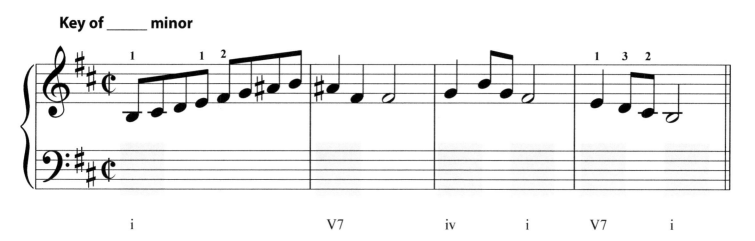

   i   V7   iv   i   V7   i

Lead Sheets

The "lead" refers to the melody. A **LEAD SHEET** consists of a melody, with chord symbols written above the melody.

1. Play each right hand melody below.

2. To create your own arrangement, add the left hand chords using the chord symbols above the melody. Use smooth chord progressions.

Lavender's Blue

Folk Melody

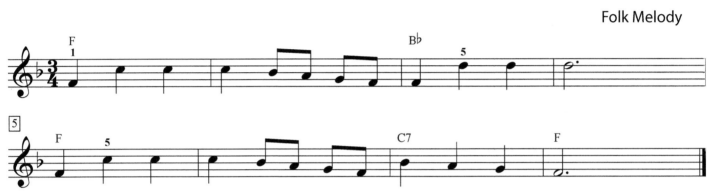

Theme from "The New World" Symphony
Second Movement (Largo)

Antonin Dvorak
(1841-1904)

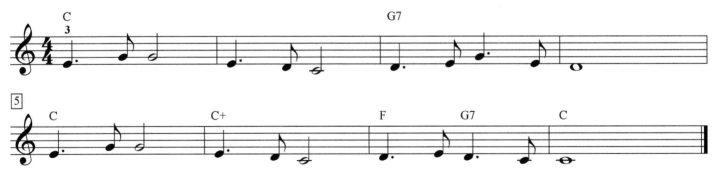

Musical Signs and Terms

An asterisk (*) indicates words that are new to this book.

The following terms help describe the mood or style of the music.

Italian Name	Meaning
allargando	growing broader and slower
espressivo	expressively
poco a poco	little by little
sempre	always
subito	suddenly
cantabile*	in a singing style
leggiero*	lightly
scherzando*	playful
senza*	without
loco*	play as written

1. In the blanks, write the definition for each term.

sempre _____   leggiero _____

espressivo _____   cantabile _____

senza _____   allargando _____

scherzando _____   poco a poco _____

loco _____   subito _____

ARTICULATION signs tell how to play and release the keys.

Name	Sign (Symbol)	Meaning
martellato		short and accented

TEMPO marks tell what speed to play the music.

Italian Name	Meaning
rallentando	slowing the tempo
piu mosso	more motion; quicker
meno mosso	less motion; slower
con brio	with spirit
con moto	with motion
lento*	slow; slower than *adagio*
vivo*	lively, bright
grave*	slow, solemn

2. Write the definition for each Italian tempo mark.

con brio _____   rallentando _____

vivo _____   meno mosso _____

lento _____   con moto _____

grave _____   piu mosso _____

Other Musical Symbols

 Coda sign means to skip to the *Coda* (ending section).

D.C. al Coda means to return to the beginning and play to ⊕, then skip to the *Coda* (ending section).

D.S. al Coda means to return to the 𝄋 and play to ⊕, then skip to the *Coda* (ending section).

15ma   **Quindicesima*** means to play two octaves higher, or lower, than written.

 **Arpeggio***   A chord whose pitches are played in succession; harp-like

REVIEW

1. Match each term or symbol with its definition by writing the correct letter in the blank.

_____ leggiero   a. slowing the tempo

_____ grave   b. coda

_____ 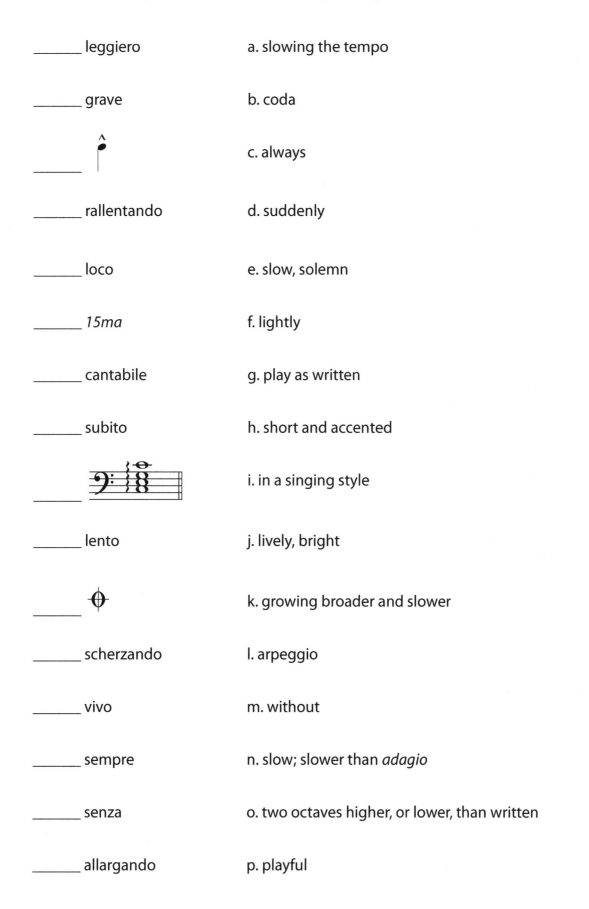   c. always

_____ rallentando   d. suddenly

_____ loco   e. slow, solemn

_____ *15ma*   f. lightly

_____ cantabile   g. play as written

_____ subito   h. short and accented

_____   i. in a singing style

_____ lento   j. lively, bright

_____   k. growing broader and slower

_____ scherzando   l. arpeggio

_____ vivo   m. without

_____ sempre   n. slow; slower than *adagio*

_____ senza   o. two octaves higher, or lower, than written

_____ allargando   p. playful

2. Write the number of sixteenth notes that equals each note value.

a. ♩ = _____

b. 𝅗𝅥 = _____

c. ♪ = _____

d. ♪. = _____

e. 𝅗𝅥. = _____

f. 𝅝 = _____

3. In each box draw one note to complete the measure.

4. Complete the linear Circle of Fifths.

Down by Perfect 5ths ⟵_____   _____⟶ Up by Perfect 5ths

C

___ ___ ___ ___ ___ ___ ___ ___ ___ ___ ___ ___ ___ ___

5. Name the order of sharps.

_____ _____ _____ _____ _____ _____ _____

6. Name the order of flats.

_____ _____ _____ _____ _____ _____ _____

7. Write the letter name in the blanks for these Major key signatures.

8. Add the sharps or flats needed to form these Major scales.

B Major

G♭ Major

C♯ Major

A♭ Major

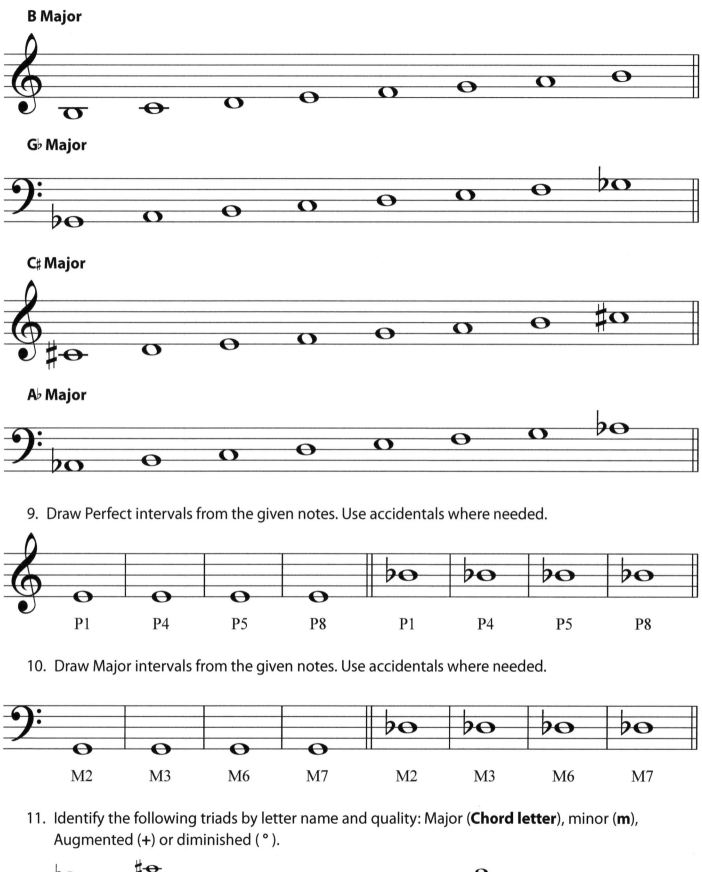

9. Draw Perfect intervals from the given notes. Use accidentals where needed.

P1   P4   P5   P8   P1   P4   P5   P8

10. Draw Major intervals from the given notes. Use accidentals where needed.

M2   M3   M6   M7   M2   M3   M6   M7

11. Identify the following triads by letter name and quality: Major (**Chord letter**), minor (**m**),
Augmented (**+**) or diminished (**°**).

12. Label each cadence as Authentic, Plagal or Half.

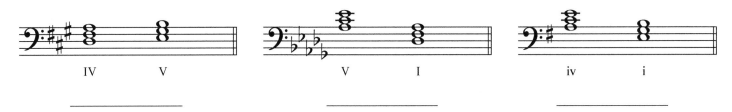

    IV   V   V   I   iv   i

_____   _____   _____

13. Label the following chord progressions with the correct Roman numerals.

Key of B♭ Major

Key of E minor

14. Build the V7 chord in root position, starting on the dominant note in each key.

15. Complete each chord progression by drawing the V7 chord in 1st inversion with the 5th omitted. *The top note of each chord will share a common tone.*

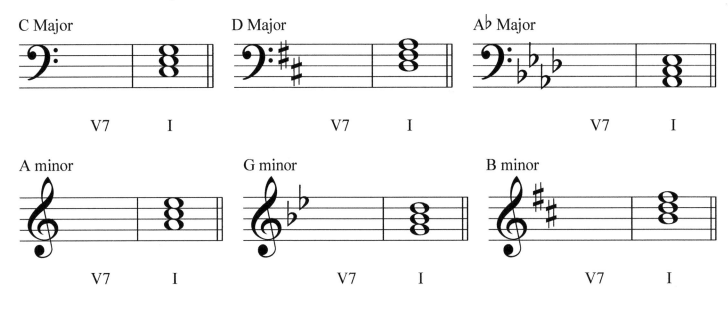

MUSICAL MASTERY

Ear Training

1. You will hear one rhythm from each pair. Circle the rhythm you hear.

2. You will hear the following intervals played in broken and blocked form: M2, M3, P5, M7 and P8. Name the interval by type and size in each blank.

    1. _____   2. _____   3. _____   4. _____   5. _____   6. _____

3. You will hear four measures of melodic dictation. Fill in the blank measures with the notes and rhythms you hear.

1. Fill in the blanks for each sentence on page 43, then complete the crossword puzzle below.

Musical Crossword Puzzle

Across

5. A chord built on the _____ note of the scale is called a dominant chord.

7. The IV – I chord progression is called a _____ cadence.

8. Another name for the fourth note of a scale is _____.

11. A minor scale with a raised 6th and 7th ascending is called a _____ minor scale.

14. $\frac{3}{4}$, $\frac{4}{4}$ and $\frac{6}{8}$ are examples of _____ _____.

16. In a major scale, the interval between the tonic note and the 2nd, 3rd, 6th and 7th is called a _____ interval.

17. The V – I chord progression is called an _____ cadence.

19. The A _____ scale has no sharps or flats.

21. To build a _____ chord, lower the third and fifth of a Major chord a half step.

22. _____ _____ is another name for $\frac{2}{2}$.

23. The interval between the tonic note and the unison, 4th, 5th and 8th is called a _____ interval.

Down

1. The _____ inversion has the letter name of the chord as the middle note.

2. To build an _____ chord, raise the fifth of a Major chord a half step.

3. To build a minor chord, lower the _____ of a Major chord a half step.

4. The sharps or flats found right after the clef sign is called the _____ _____.

5. The E♭ Major scale has three _____.

6. A _____ is the combination of chords that ends a phrase or section of music.

9. When the notes of a chord are all on lines or all in spaces, the chord is in _____ position.

10. The I, IV and V chords are the _____ _____ of a Major scale.

12. The order of sharps is _____ _____ _____ _____ _____ _____ _____ .

13. _____ _____ is another name for $\frac{4}{4}$.

15. Another name for the first note of a scale is _____ .

18. A minor scale with a raised seventh is called a _____ minor scale.

20. A 7th chord built on the 5th degree of the scale is called a _____ 7th chord.

Analysis

Study this excerpt from "The Avalanche," then answer the questions about it.

The Avalanche
Op. 45, No. 2

Stephen Heller
(1813–1888)

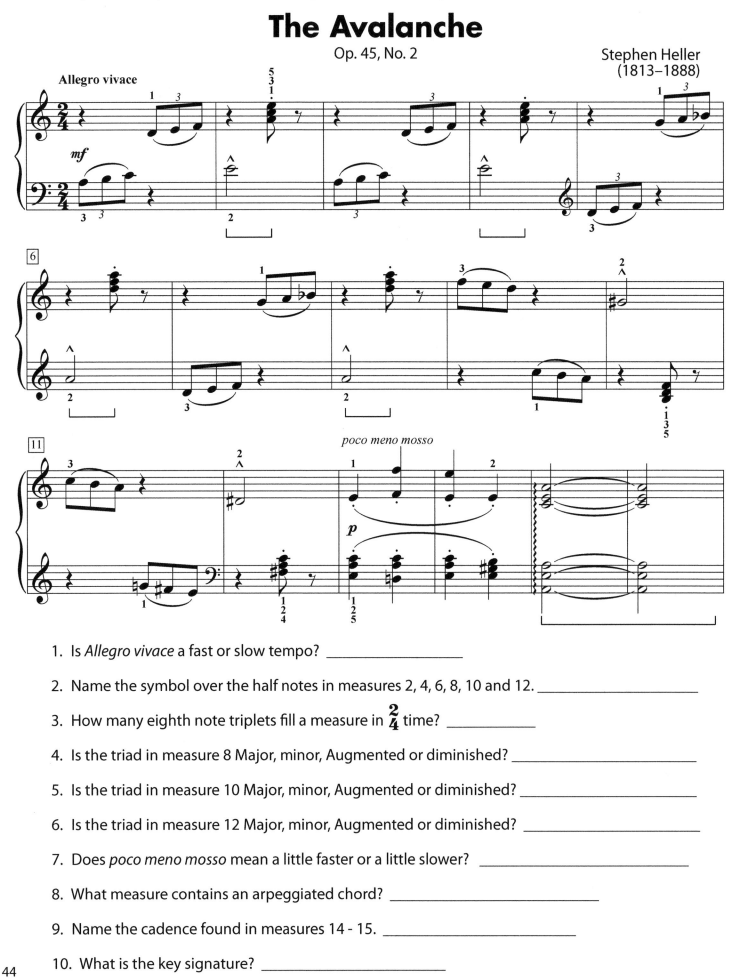

1. Is *Allegro vivace* a fast or slow tempo? _____

2. Name the symbol over the half notes in measures 2, 4, 6, 8, 10 and 12. _____

3. How many eighth note triplets fill a measure in $\frac{2}{4}$ time? _____

4. Is the triad in measure 8 Major, minor, Augmented or diminished? _____

5. Is the triad in measure 10 Major, minor, Augmented or diminished? _____

6. Is the triad in measure 12 Major, minor, Augmented or diminished? _____

7. Does *poco meno mosso* mean a little faster or a little slower? _____

8. What measure contains an arpeggiated chord? _____

9. Name the cadence found in measures 14 - 15. _____

10. What is the key signature? _____

44

THEORY MASTERY

Review Test

1. Draw bar lines where they are needed.

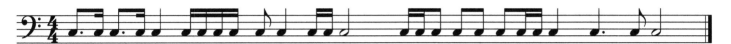

2. Add all the notes and rests as you would count them in $\frac{4}{4}$ time. Write the total number of beats in each box.

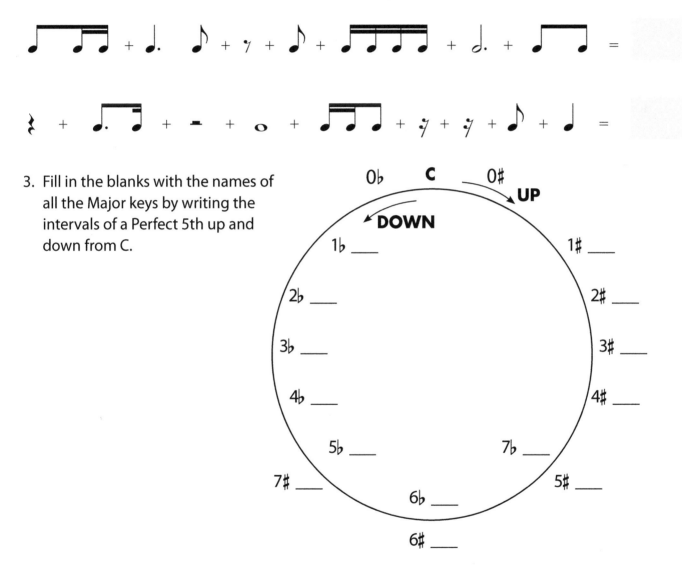

3. Fill in the blanks with the names of all the Major keys by writing the intervals of a Perfect 5th up and down from C.

0♭   C   0♯
UP
DOWN

1♭ ___   1♯ ___

2♭ ___   2♯ ___

3♭ ___   3♯ ___

4♭ ___   4♯ ___

5♭ ___   7♭ ___

7♯ ___   5♯ ___

6♭ ___

6♯ ___

4. Draw the seven sharps in order on the correct lines and spaces.

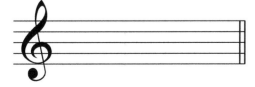

5. Draw the seven flats in order on the correct lines and spaces.

6. Identify each interval as P1, M2, M3, P4, P5, M6, M7 or P8.

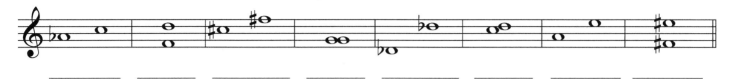

_____ _____ _____ _____ _____ _____ _____ _____ _____ _____

7. Draw the note that completes the harmonic interval above the given note. Add accidentals where needed.

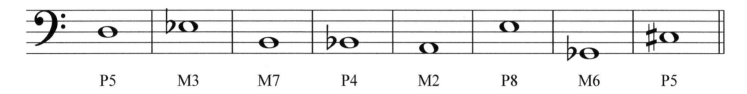

P5   M3   M7   P4   M2   P8   M6   P5

8. Build Major, minor, Augmented or diminished triads in root position on each given note.

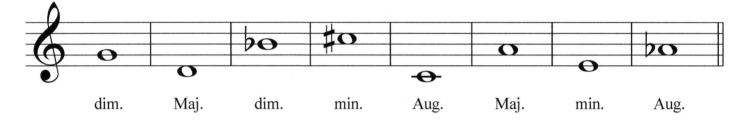

dim.   Maj.   dim.   min.   Aug.   Maj.   min.   Aug.

9. In the blanks, identify the Roman numerals for each chord. In the boxes, label each cadence as Authentic, Plagal or Half.

C Major   Eb Major

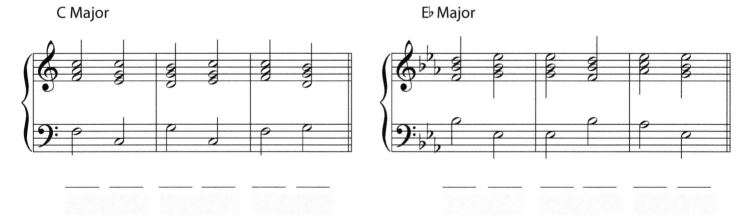

_____ _____ _____ _____   _____ _____ _____ _____

10. Write the following Dominant 7th (V7) chords in root position in the given key signatures.

A Major   Db Major   E Major   D minor   E minor   A minor

SYMBOL MASTERY

Unscramble the words to complete each sentence.

1. Another name for $\frac{4}{4}$ is _____ _____.
   momnco   meti

2. Another name for $\frac{2}{4}$ is _____ _____.
   utc   tmei

3. The key of C♭ Major has _____ flats.
   vesne

4. Keys are related by _____ 5ths.
   ftecrep

5. _____ keys sound the same, but are written differently.
   crehnainmo

6. The interval between the tonic note and the 2nd, 3rd, 6th and 7th is called a _____
   interval.   arjom

7. A _____ triad is made up of two minor thirds.
   minhdiesdi

8. An _____ triad is made up of two Major thirds.
   tgeamunde

9. The combination of chords that ends a phrase or section of music is called a

   _____.
   decacen

10. A dominant seventh chord has _____ inversions.
    herte

11. _____ tones are notes shared between chords in a progression.
    onmcmo

12. A _____ _____ consists of a melody with chord symbols written above it.
    alde   ehste

13. The key of C♯ Major has seven _____.
    hasrsp

EAR TRAINING

1. You will hear four measures of rhythmic dictation. Fill in the blank measures with the rhythm you hear.

2. You will hear six triads played in broken and blocked form. Identify them as Major, minor or diminished.

   1. _____   2. _____   3. _____

   4. _____   5. _____   6. _____

3. Listen to the following chord progressions. Circle the one you hear from each pair.

   a.   I   IV   V7   I

                    or

       I   IV   I   V7

   b.   i   V7   i   iv

                    or

       i   iv   V7   i

4. You will hear four measures of melodic dictation. Fill in the blank measures with the notes and rhythms you hear.

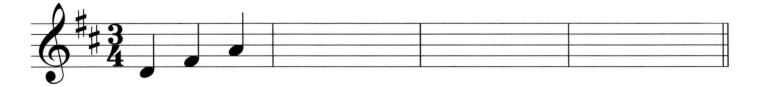